CATtastic CRAFTS

Cattastic Crafts
Published in 2016 by Zakka Workshop,
a division of World Book Media LLC

www.zakkaworkshop.com
134 Federal Street
Salem, MA 01970 USA
info@zakkaworkshop.com

Copyright © 2009 Boutique-Sha.
KANTA N! KAWAI! NEKO GUZZU INTERIA NI MO NARU, NEKO GUZZU GA IPPAI!
Originally published in Japanese language by Boutique-Sha, Tokyo, Japan
English language rights, translation & production by Zakka Workshop
English Editor: Lindsay Fair
Translator: Kyoko Matthews

ISBN: 978-1-940552-26-2

Printed in China
10 9 8 7 6 5 4 3 2 1

CATtastic CRAFTS

DIY Projects for Cats and Cat People

Mariko Ishikawa

INTRODUCTION

I have seven cats. Yes, you read that correctly: seven cats. Living with so many cats, I've learned that each and every one possesses their own unique personality. Each cat has his or her own favorite toys, favorite nap spots, and favorite games.

I've also learned that it's very important to provide cats with their "creature comforts" to keep them happy.

Pet stores offer a nearly endless supply of cat products, but I've never been satisfied with the items I've purchased for my cats. The well-made items are often very expensive, while the affordable options fall apart after only one or two uses. Plus, it's difficult to find storage solutions, feeding stations, and cat furniture that work well with the décor of your home.

This dilemma inspired me to create a book full of ideas for quick and easy DIY cat projects. All of the designs in this book use inexpensive, easy-to-find materials, such as cardboard boxes, plywood, and felt. I hope you and your feline friends enjoy this collection of toys, beds, clothing, and more!

–Mariko Ishikawa

Meet the Models

We are two of Mariko's cats!

Chai
2 year old male
I enjoy taking naps in my spare time.

Latte
2 year old male
I am one very curious little cat.

CONTENTS

CATNIP MOUSE

This little mouse is made with a soft, fuzzy sock, then filled with cotton stuffing and some catnip. Don't forget to attach an attention-getting tail made with ribbon or faux fur. The catnip-laced stuffing makes this toy extra exciting!

The fur tail is my favorite

Materials

Gray Mouse

- One marshmallow texture gray sock
- Gray, brown, and black felt
- 4"–8" (10–20 cm) of pink faux fur trim
- Cotton stuffing
- Catnip
- Needle and thread

White Mouse

- One marshmallow texture white sock
- Pink and black felt
- 4"–8" (10–20 cm) of white lace ribbon
- Cotton stuffing
- Catnip
- Needle and thread

Instructions

1. Sprinkle catnip onto a handful of cotton stuffing. Insert the stuffing into the foot of the sock. Fold the ankle inside the foot of the sock.

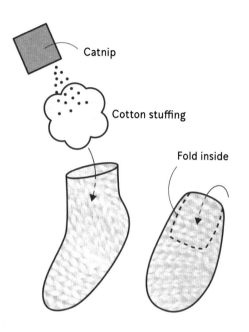

Catnip

Cotton stuffing

Fold inside

2. Sew around the opening, then pull the thread taut to squeeze the sock closed. Tie a knot and trim the thread. Sew the faux fur trim or lace ribbon to the end of the sock.

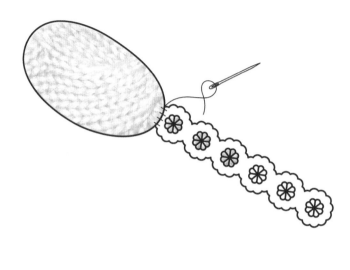

3. Use the templates on page 91 to cut the nose, eyes, and ears out of felt. Sew the felt pieces to the other end of the sock to make a face.

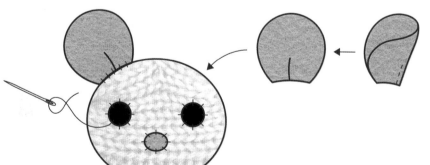

Fold each ear in half. Make 2-3 stitches. Unfold and sew the bottom of the ear to the sock.

More catnip please!

Does your dryer eat socks? Since this toy is made with only one sock, it's the perfect way to use up all of the orphan socks you have lying around.

Experiment with different colors and sizes of socks. Kids socks are the perfect size to make miniature mice!

FAN-TASTIC TEASER

Drive your kitty wild with this super easy-to-make fan teaser.
Embellish an inexpensive paper paddle fan with some ribbon
and a few shiny plastic streamers, then watch the cat
gymnastics ensue!

Materials

- One Japanese paddle fan

- Seven 16"–20" (40–50 cm) long
  pieces of sheer pink ribbon

- Two 16"–20" (40–50 cm) long pieces each
  of yellow and green metallic ribbon

- Yellow, pink, black, and white construction paper

- Glue

- Duct tape

Instructions

1. Trace the outline of the fan onto the yellow construction paper. Cut out along the traced lines.

2. Glue the yellow construction paper to the fan. Use the templates on page 91 to cut the mouth, nose, eyes, and ears out of construction paper. Glue the felt pieces to the fan to make a face.

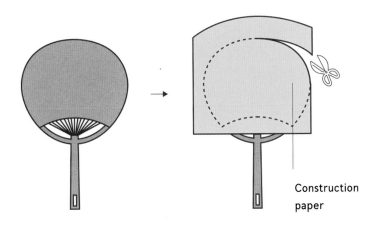

Construction paper

3. Glue the pieces of ribbon to the back of the fan. Use a strip of duct tape to hold the pieces of ribbon in place on the back of the fan.

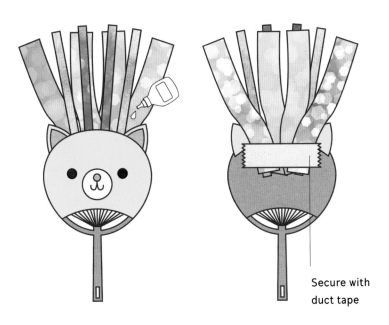

Secure with duct tape

CRINKLE CRITTERS

There is nothing that captures a cat's attention quite like the sound of crinkling plastic. Made from plastic bags, these crinkle toys are super easy and quick to make. There are two designs to choose from—a butterfly on a string for dangling and a "toss and attack" cat face.

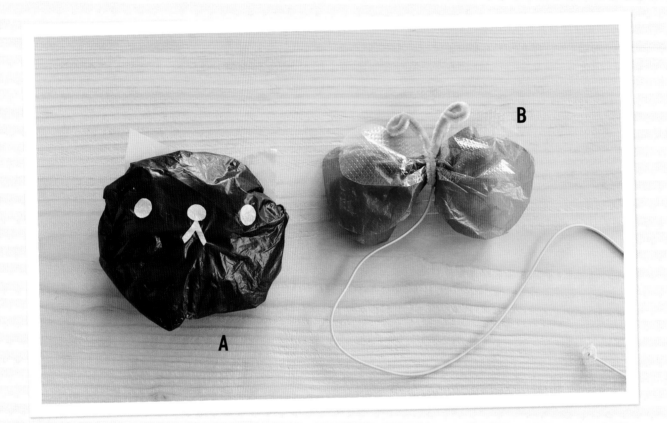

Materials

For A

- Light brown, dark brown, and white plastic bags
- Tape
- Double-sided scrapbooking tape

For B

- Red, blue, and clear plastics bags
- One green pipe cleaner
- One 12"–16" (30–40 cm) long piece of ¹⁄₁₆" (2 mm) round elastic cord

Instructions for A

1. Crumple the dark brown plastic bag into a ball. Use pieces of tape to hold the ball together.

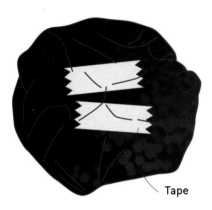

Tape

2. Adhere pieces of double-sided scrapbooking tape to the light brown and white plastic bags. Use the templates on page 92 to cut out the nose, eyes, and ears from the portions of the bags with the double-sided scrapbooking tape. Peel the paper off the double-sided scrapbooking tape and adhere the pieces to the ball to make a face.

Instructions for B

1. Use the template on page 92 to cut a butterfly out of each plastic bag.

2. Layer the three butterflies on top of each other in the following order: clear, red, blue. Twist the pipe cleaner around the center to bind the butterflies together. Wrap the ends of the pipe cleaner around a pencil to create the antennae.

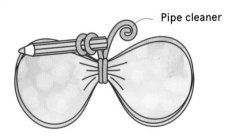

Pipe cleaner

3. Tie the piece of elastic to the pipe cleaner.

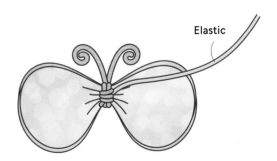

Elastic

TINFOIL TEASERS

For a low-budget toy, crumple some aluminum foil into balls, then string onto yarn. Cats will be mesmerized by the rattle and crinkle of the foil. Use non-toxic markers to add some extra color and shimmer, then let the games begin: Rattle, toss, and watch for the big POUNCE.

Materials

For All

- Aluminum foil
- Toothpick
- Permanent markers in a variety of colors
- Tape

For A

- 12"–16" (30–40 cm) of orange yarn

For B and C

- 12"–16" (30–40 cm) of string each

Instructions

1. Cut several small squares of aluminum foil. Use the permanent markers to color the pieces of foil as desired.

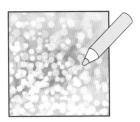

2. Crumple the pieces of foil into balls.

3. Tape the yarn or string to the toothpick. Insert the toothpick through each foil ball to string them onto the yarn or string.

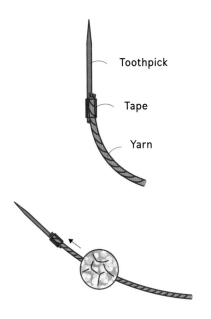

Toothpick

Tape

Yarn

4. Once all the foil balls have been strung together, tie the ends of the yarn or string into a knot.

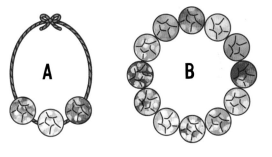

A   B

GO FISH TEASER

Go fishing with this teaser and you'll catch a very playful cat. Use an old towel or scrap of terrycloth for the fish body and a bouncy elastic cord for the line. Attach a little bell inside the fish's mouth for extra fun. Swing the rod and the line will bounce around, ringing the little bell—you may be surprised how high your cat will jump!

Materials

- Pink washcloth

- Red and blue felt

- Green rubber band

- One clear plastic capsule

- Bell

- 1 yard (1 m) of ⅛" (3 mm) round blue elastic cord

- One ⅜" x 12" (1 x 30 cm) dowel

- Needle and thread

Instructions

1. Use the template on page 92 to cut the dorsal fin out of felt. Tie a knot at one end of the elastic cord. Fold the washcloth in half with the fin and elastic sandwiched in between. Sew the washcloth together along two sides. Stitch over the elastic a few times to ensure that it is attached securely.

Elastic cord

Washcloth

2. Turn the washcloth right side out. Put the bell inside the plastic capsule, then insert into the fish.

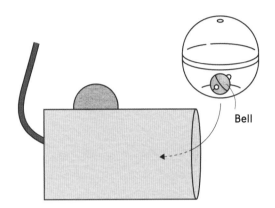

Bell

3. Wrap the rubber band around the washcloth to close the open end. Tuck the two corners in as shown below.

Tuck inside

Rubber band

4. Push on the seam to form the mouth. Pinch two layers of fabric together and sew around the mouth in a circle. Use the templates on page 92 to cut the eyes, pectoral fins, and stomach fins out of felt. Sew the fins and eyes to the fish.

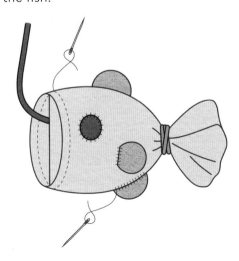

CAT NAP PILLOWS

Perfect for an afternoon nap, these cat-sized body pillows are made from knit headbands and scrunchies. For added coziness, look for headbands and scrunchies made from soft materials, such as terrycloth or velour. Simply cut the fabric open, insert stuffing, and then sew the ends closed. If you really want to drive your cat wild, try adding a pinch of catnip to the stuffing.

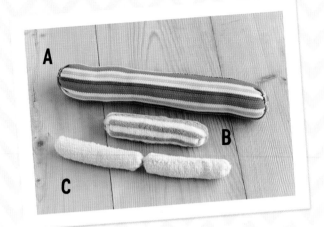

Materials

- Cotton stuffing
- Catnip
- One knit headband
- Needle and thread

Instructions

1. Cut the headband to create a tube.
   For B, trim the headband to desired size.

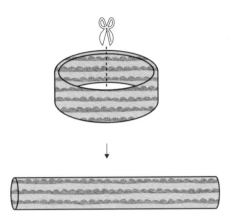

2. Sew around one end of the tube. Fold the seam allowance in, then pull the thread taut to squeeze the tube closed. Tie a knot and trim the thread.

Fold the seam allowance in

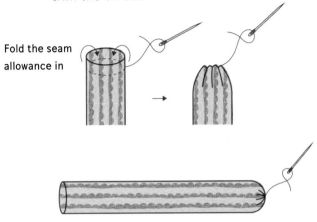

3. Sprinkle catnip onto the cotton stuffing. For A and B, fill the entire tube with the stuffing. For C, fill half of the tube with stuffing.

Catnip

Cotton stuffing

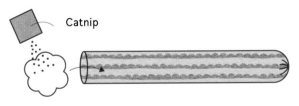

4. For A and B, repeat step 2 to sew the other end of the tube closed. For C, sew around the center of the tube, then pull the thread taut to squeeze the tube closed. Tie a knot and trim the thread. Fill the rest of the tube with stuffing, then repeat step 2 to sew the other end of the tube closed.

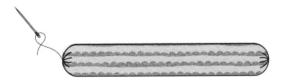

FINGER TEASERS

These unique cat teasers are the perfect way to upcycle mismatched, stray gloves. Cut the fingers from one glove and attach them to the tips of another for a fluttering teaser your cat will love. You can even decorate individual teasers with googly eyes, ribbons, and streamers. Attach one of these decked out fingers to your glove for additional fun. Just watch your fingers please!

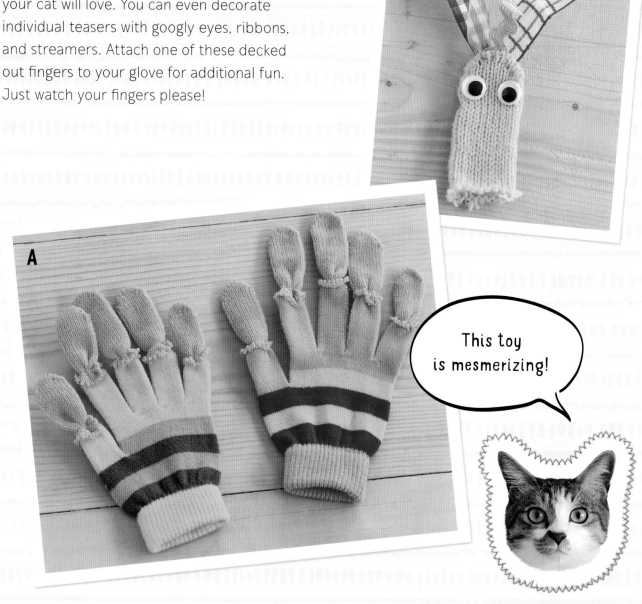

B

A

This toy is mesmerizing!

Materials

For A

- Two pairs of knit gloves

- Needle and thread

For B

- One knit glove

- Four 2" (5 cm) long ribbons

- Two ⅜" (1 cm) googly eyes

- Needle and thread

- Glue

Instructions for A

1. Cut the fingers off of one glove.

2. Sew the fingers to the tips of another glove.

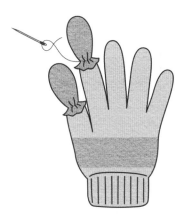

Instructions for B

1. Apply a ring of glue to the glove around the base of the middle finger. Let the glue dry completely. This will prevent the fabric from fraying. Once the glue is dry, cut the finger off of the glove along the glue line.

2. Sew the ribbons to the fingertip. Glue the googly eyes to the finger.

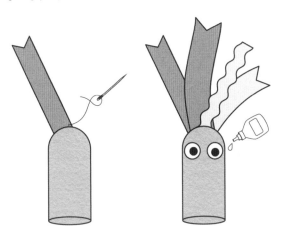

THE CAT CHATEAU

This adorable hide-and-seek house is made from a discarded cardboard box, so your cat is sure to love it! Decorate the outside with colorful fabric and felt. Add a fleece cushion inside for a cozy, happy space any cat would be proud to call home.

Materials

- One cardboard box (the one used here measured 13" L x 16" W x 9 ½" H [32 x 40 x 24 cm])

- One piece of flat cardboard (the one used here measured 13" x 16" [32 x 40 cm])

- Red striped fabric: Two 9 ½" x 13" (24 x 32 cm) pieces

- Blue striped fabric: Two 9 ½" x 16" (24 x 40 cm) pieces

- Orange fleece: Two 6 ¼" x 13" (16 x 32 cm) pieces and two 6 ¼" x 16" (16 x 40 cm) pieces

- Green fleece: One 13" x 16" (32 x 40 cm) piece

- 2 ¾ yards (2.5 m) of ⅝" (1.5 cm) wide white lace

- Light blue, yellow, and pink felt

- Utility knife

- Glue

- Tape

Instructions

1. Use a utility knife to cut out the windows. Next, trim the top flaps of the box at an angle to make the roof slanted.

Tip: Place a cutting mat or a scrap of cardboard inside the box so you don't damage your work surface or accidentally cut a part of the box that shouldn't be cut.

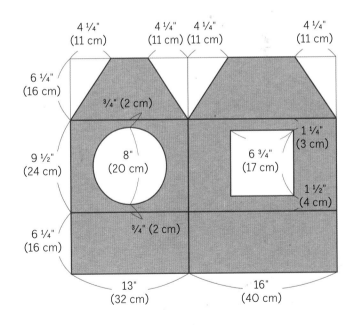

2. Trace the outline of the walls and windows onto the wrong side of the striped fabrics. Cut out along the traced lines. Glue the fabric to the cardboard.

3. Tape the flat piece of cardboard to the inside bottom of the box. Glue the piece of green fleece to the flat piece of cardboard.

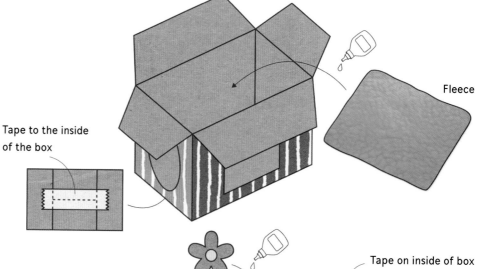

Fleece

Tape to the inside of the box

4. Fold the roof into place and tape together on the inside of the box. Glue the lace to the roof. Use the templates on page 93 to cut the flowers out of felt. Glue the flowers to the box.

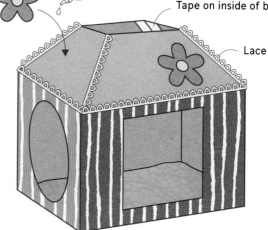

Tape on inside of box

Lace

GIRAFFE CAT TOWER

This cat tower has it all: It includes three multi-level climbing platforms, a giraffe-shaped scratching post, a cozy hammock, and storage for hiding away all those cat toys! The three climbing platforms are different heights and can be configured several different ways. Separate the platforms and create a series of surfaces to jump on, perch, and play. You'll also love how easily and compactly they can be stacked and stowed out of the way.

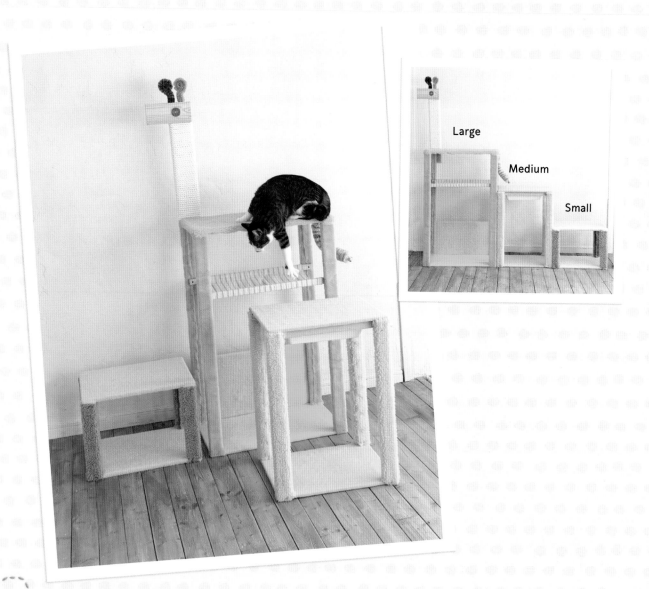

A. Attach sisal rope and scrubbing brushes to a piece of wood to create a scratching post.

B. A comfy hammock stretches just underneath the tallest of the three platforms. Cozy!

C. The medium-sized platform includes a storage drawer, ideal for hiding away toys.

D. All three platforms can be stacked and stored inside each other!

Materials for Small Platform

- Plywood: Dimensions noted in step 1
- Dimensional lumber: Dimensions noted in step 1
- White faux shearling fabric: About ¾ yard (0.7 m)
- Blue faux shearling fabric: About ¾ yard (0.7 m)
- Table saw or circular saw (for cutting plywood)
- Hand saw (for cutting dimensional lumber)
- Drill and wood screws or hammer and nails
- Utility knife
- Wood glue or strong adhesive

Instructions

1. Use the table or circular saw to cut the top and bottom out of plywood. Use the hand saw to cut four legs out of dimensional lumber.

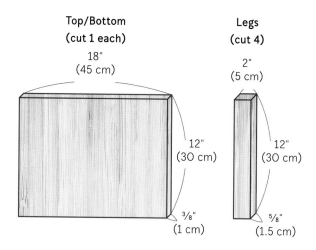

Top/Bottom
(cut 1 each)
18" (45 cm)
12" (30 cm)
³⁄₈" (1 cm)

Legs
(cut 4)
2" (5 cm)
12" (30 cm)
⁵⁄₈" (1.5 cm)

2. Use the drill and wood screws or hammer and nails to attach a leg to each corner of the bottom. Once all four legs are in place, attach the top.

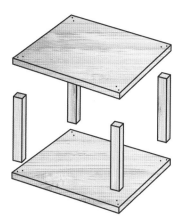

3. Glue pieces of white faux shearling fabric to the top and bottom and pieces of blue faux shearling fabric to the legs.

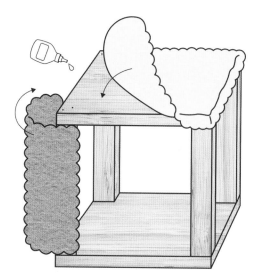

Materials for Medium Platform

- Plywood: Dimensions noted in step 1

- Dimensional lumber: Dimensions noted in step 1

- Pink faux shearling fabric: About ¾ yard (0.7 m)

- Pink fleece: About ¾ yard (0.7 m)

- Two 16 ½" L x ⅞" W (42 x 2.2 cm) plastic L-shaped brackets

- One 16" x 9 ½" x 2" (40 x 24 x 2 cm) plastic bin

- Table saw or circular saw (for cutting plywood)

- Hand saw (for cutting dimensional lumber)

- Drill and wood screws or hammer and nails

- Utility knife

- Wood glue or strong adhesive

- Heavy-duty double-sided tape

Instructions

1. Use the table or circular saw to cut the top and bottom (A) out of plywood. Use the hand saw to cut four legs (B) and two drawers (C) out of dimensional lumber.

2. Refer to step 2 on page 28 to assemble the medium platform following the same process used to assemble the small platform.

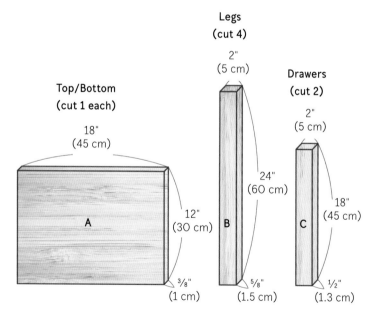

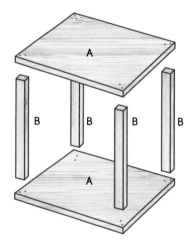

3. Adhere a piece of double-sided tape to each L-shaped bracket. Next, adhere each bracket to a C piece, leaving about ¾" (1.5 cm) on each end.

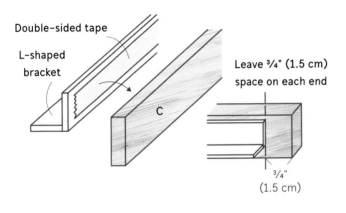

Double-sided tape

L-shaped bracket

C

Leave ¾" (1.5 cm) space on each end

¾" (1.5 cm)

4. Use the drill and wood screws or hammer and nails to attach the C pieces from step 3 to the inside of the platform, just beneath the top. Insert the plastic bin into the brackets to complete the drawer. Use the pink fleece to cover the top and bottom (A) and the sides of the C pieces. Use the pink faux shearling to cover the legs (B).

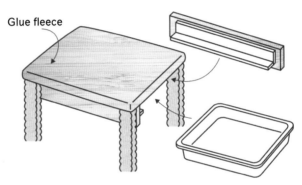

Glue fleece

So that's where all of my toys have been hiding!

Materials for Large Platform

- Plywood: Dimensions noted in step 1

- Dimensional lumber: Dimensions noted in step 1

- Yellow faux shearling fabric: About ½ yard (0.5 m)

- Green faux shearling fabric: About ¾ yard (0.7 m)

- Yellow fleece: About ¾ yard (0.7 m)

- Red striped fabric: One 17" x 22" (43 x 56 cm) piece

- Japanese scrubbing brushes in brown, beige, and beige stripe

- One bell

- One 1 ½" (4 cm) button

- 5 ½ yards (5 m) of ⅜" (9 mm) round sisal rope

- Table saw or circular saw (for cutting plywood)

- Hand saw (for cutting dimensional lumber)

- Drill and wood screws or hammer and nails

- Utility knife

- Wood glue or strong adhesive

Instructions

1. Use the table or circular saw to cut the three A pieces out of plywood. These will be the top, bottom, and back. Use the hand saw to cut pieces B–E out of dimensional lumber.

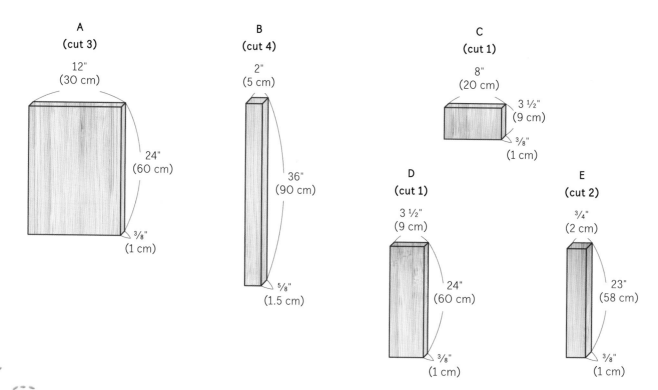

A
(cut 3)
12"
(30 cm)
24"
(60 cm)
⅜"
(1 cm)

B
(cut 4)
2"
(5 cm)
36"
(90 cm)
⅝"
(1.5 cm)

C
(cut 1)
8"
(20 cm)
3 ½"
(9 cm)
⅜"
(1 cm)

D
(cut 1)
3 ½"
(9 cm)
24"
(60 cm)
⅜"
(1 cm)

E
(cut 2)
¾"
(2 cm)
23"
(58 cm)
⅜"
(1 cm)

2. Refer to step 2 on page 28 to assemble the large platform following the same process used to assemble the small platform. Use the yellow fleece to cover the bottom (A), the yellow faux shearling to cover the top (A), and the green faux shearling to cover the legs (B). Cover the back (the remaining A piece) with yellow fleece. Working from the wrong side, screw A to the back legs. Make the hammock, giraffe head, and giraffe tail as shown below.

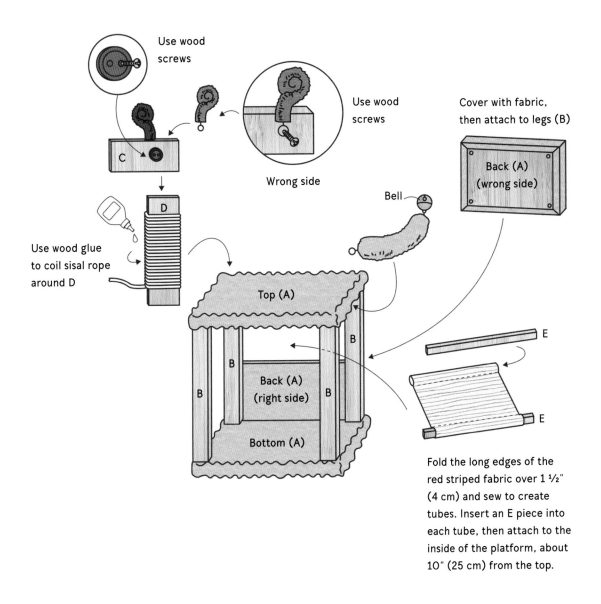

Use wood screws

Use wood screws

Cover with fabric, then attach to legs (B)

Back (A) (wrong side)

C

Wrong side

Bell

Use wood glue to coil sisal rope around D

D

Top (A)

B

B

B

B

Back (A) (right side)

Bottom (A)

E

E

Fold the long edges of the red striped fabric over 1 ½" (4 cm) and sew to create tubes. Insert an E piece into each tube, then attach to the inside of the platform, about 10" (25 cm) from the top.

CONVERTIBLE CAT BED

This soft fleece cat bed can be used as a flat resting mat or bed. Strategically placed ribbons allow you to tie up the mat corners to create snug and cozy little walls, making this a safe space for a sleepy cat. Decorate the bed with felt ears, eyes, and a mouth so it looks like a little cat—and so everyone knows it's kitty's special spot!

This mat transforms
into a cat bed!

This fleece bed
is so cozy!

Materials

- 51 ¼" x 63" (130 x 160 cm) of light blue fleece

- 29 ½" x 39 ½" (75 x 100 cm) of thick quilt batting

- Two 12" (30 cm) square pieces of blue felt

- One 12" (30 cm) square piece of purple felt

- Two 31 ½" (80 cm) long yellow ribbons

- Two 31 ½" (80 cm) long purple ribbons

Instructions

1. Layer the quilt batting on top of the fleece. Fold the fleece in half.

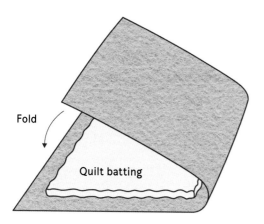

Fold

Quilt batting

2. Make the ears out of blue felt. Insert each ear between the two layers of fleece. Sew around three sides of the fleece as indicated by the dotted line in the diagram below. Don't forget to sew the corners into a rounded shape.

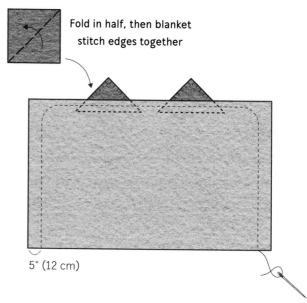

Fold in half, then blanket stitch edges together

5" (12 cm)

3. Trim the corners into a rounded shape. Use the templates on page 92 to cut the eyes and nose out of purple felt. Sew the felt pieces to the fleece to make a face.

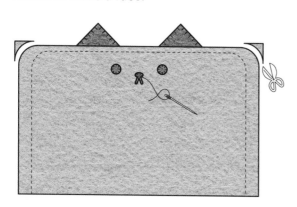

4. Turn the mat over to the wrong side. Sew a piece of ribbon to each corner by stitching along the center of each ribbon.

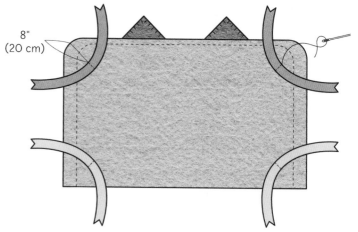

8" (20 cm)

CHILL BASKET

Does your cat end up napping in your fruit basket and other inconvenient places? Every cat needs his or her own little space, and this quick project offers the perfect solution. Line an inexpensive plastic basket with a piece of fun fabric, then add a decorative ribbon bow. We promise that your cat is sure to love this cozy little perch.

Materials

- 12" (31 cm) diameter basket
- 21 ¾" x 21 ¾" (55 x 55 cm) of floral print fabric
- 59" (150 cm) of ¾" (2 cm) wide ribbon
- Double-sided tape

- Glue
- Pinking shears
- Needle and thread

Instructions

1. Adhere a couple of pieces of double-sided tape to the bottom of the basket. Trim the edges of the fabric using pinking shears in order to prevent them from fraying.

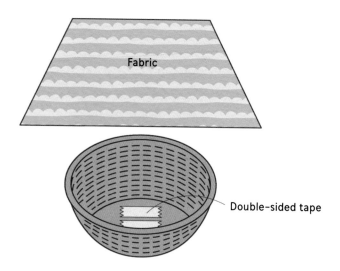

Fabric

Double-sided tape

2. Cover the basket with the fabric. Arrange the fabric so that the portion that drapes over the edges of the basket is equal on all sides.

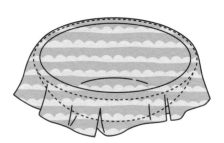

3. Sew the fabric to the basket by stitching through the holes in the basketweave. Position your stitches just under the rim of the basket. If your basket doesn't have holes, just glue the fabric in place.

4. Wrap the ribbon around the basket and tie a bow. Glue the ribbon to the fabric, covering the stitches from step 3.

FAIRY TALE BED

This adorable wooden bed is fit for a fairy tale feline—it makes the perfect spot for a catnap or an evening of beauty sleep. Use the included templates to stencil decorative motifs onto the wood, or freehand your own designs.

Materials

- Plywood: Dimensions noted in step 1 on page 40

- Dimensional lumber: Dimensions noted in step 1 on page 40

- 1 ¼" (3 cm) diameter dowel

- Table or circular saw (for cutting plywood)

- Hand saw (for cutting dimensional lumber and dowel)

- Drill and wood screws or hammer and nails

- Wood glue or strong adhesive

- Blank stencil sheet

- Paint

- Sponge

- Paintbrush

Instructions

1. Use the table or circular saw to cut the bottom (A) out of plywood. Use the hand saw to cut the B and C pieces out of dimensional lumber and the legs out of the dowel.

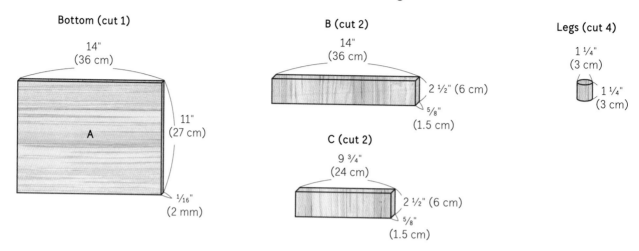

Bottom (cut 1)

14"
(36 cm)

A

11"
(27 cm)

1/16"
(2 mm)

B (cut 2)

14"
(36 cm)

2 1/2" (6 cm)

5/8"
(1.5 cm)

C (cut 2)

9 3/4"
(24 cm)

2 1/2" (6 cm)

5/8"
(1.5 cm)

Legs (cut 4)

1 1/4"
(3 cm)

1 1/4"
(3 cm)

2. Use the drill and wood screws or hammer and nails to create a frame using the B and C pieces. Next, attach the bottom (A) to the frame.

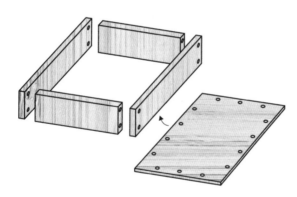

3. Glue a leg to each corner of the bottom.

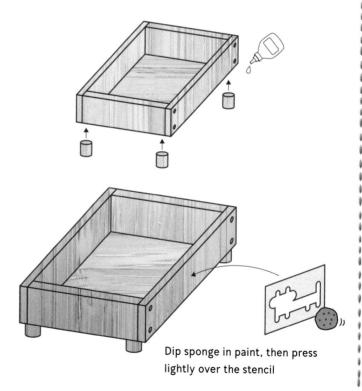

4. Create stencils using the templates on page 93. Use a sponge to dab paint onto the wood in the area outlined by the stencil. Use a paintbrush to add a nose, eyes, and whiskers to the cat.

Dip sponge in paint, then press lightly over the stencil

MOSAIC KIBBLE TRAYS

Designed with the most discerning cats in mind, these classy mosaic trays will transform unsightly food dishes into stylish home décor. Plus, these elevated feeders make mealtime more comfortable, especially for larger cats.

Materials

- Plywood: Dimensions noted in step 1 on page 42

- Dimensional lumber: Dimensions noted in step 1 on page 42

- ¾" (2 cm) diameter dowel

- Wood glue or strong adhesive

- About thirty-six ¾" (2 cm) square mosaic tiles

- Grout

- Trowel

- Table or circular saw (for cutting plywood)

- Hand saw (for cutting dimensional lumber and dowel)

Instructions

1. Use the table or circular saw to cut the base out of plywood. Use the hand saw to cut the sides out of dimensional lumber and the legs out of the dowel.

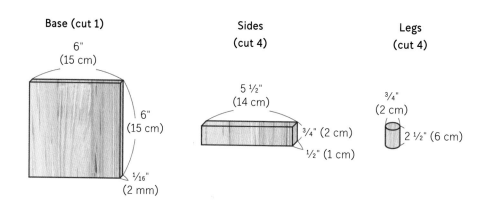

Base (cut 1)

6"
(15 cm)

6"
(15 cm)

¹⁄₁₆"
(2 mm)

Sides
(cut 4)

5 ½"
(14 cm)

¾" (2 cm)

½" (1 cm)

Legs
(cut 4)

¾"
(2 cm)

2 ½" (6 cm)

2. Glue the sides together to create a frame. Glue the frame to the plywood base.

3. Glue the tiles to the plywood base. Let the glue dry completely.

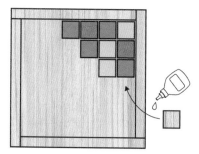

4. Use a trowel to apply grout evenly over the tile, pressing the grout into the cracks. Let the grout dry for 15–20 minutes. Use a damp towel to wipe off the excess grout.

5. Glue a leg to each corner of the base.

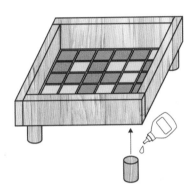

Tip: If you don't have a trowel, you can always use your hands...just make sure to wear rubber gloves!

This tray makes mealtime more comfortable for big cats like me!

WATER STATION

Transform a store-bought platter into an elegant, one-of-a-kind tray for your cat's water bowl. Simply glue short dowel pieces to the bottom of the tray, then decorate with paint and fabric. Waterproof fabric, such as vinyl or laminated cotton, makes cleanup a breeze.

Materials

- 8" x 9" (20 x 22.5 cm) tray

- Four 1 ¼" x 1 ¼" (3 x 3 cm) dowel pieces

- Hand saw (for cutting dowel)

- Wood glue or strong adhesive

- Paint

- Paintbrush

- ¼ yard (0.25 m) of vinyl or laminated cotton fabric

Instructions

1. Paint the tray and dowel pieces. Let dry completely.

2. Trace the outline of the tray onto the fabric. Cut the fabric, cutting slightly inside the traced lines so the fabric will fit inside the tray.

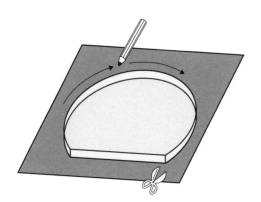

3. Glue the fabric to the tray.

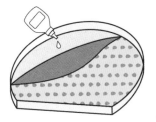

4. Glue a leg to each corner of the tray.

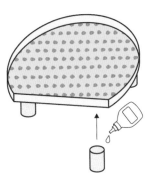

TIDY CAT STORAGE BOX

Looking for the purr-fect home for toys, food, and other cat-related items? This high-style storage solution may look complicated to construct, but it's actually quite simple: Glue a tall cardboard box to a plywood platform, then cover with fabric. Attach casters to the base to allow for easy toy cleanup.

Materials

- One cardboard box (the one used here measured 13 ½" L x 7" W x 12 ½" H [34 x 18 x 32 cm)]

- Plywood: Dimensions noted in step 1

- Table or circular saw (for cutting plywood)

- Utility knife

- Floral fabric: About 1 yard (1 m)

- Glue

- Four 1" (2.5 cm) diameter casters

- Drill and wood screws

- Orange felt

Instructions

1. Cut the top flaps off of the cardboard box. Use the table or circular saw to cut the base out of plywood.

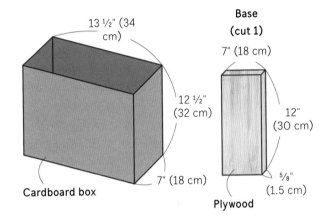

13 ½" (34 cm)

12 ½" (32 cm)

7" (18 cm)

Cardboard box

Base (cut 1)

7" (18 cm)

12" (30 cm)

⅝" (1.5 cm)

Plywood

2. Cut handle holes in the two short sides of the box. Cut a piece of fabric for each side of the box. Each piece should be 1 ½" (4 cm) longer than the height of your box. Glue the fabric to the box, folding the top ¾" (2 cm) to the inside of the box and the bottom ¾" (2 cm) to the bottom of the box. You may need to cut diagonal slits at the corners to make the fabric fold neatly beneath the bottom of the box. Mark the handle placement and cut the fabric out of those areas.

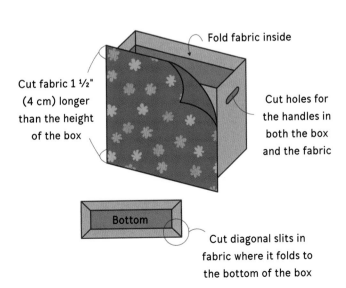

Fold fabric inside

Cut fabric 1 ½" (4 cm) longer than the height of the box

Cut holes for the handles in both the box and the fabric

Bottom

Cut diagonal slits in fabric where it folds to the bottom of the box

3. Use the drill and wood screws to attach a caster to each corner of the plywood base. Glue the plywood base to the bottom of the box.

4. Use the templates on page 94 to cut the tail and ears out of orange felt. Glue the tail and ears to the box.

Is it just me, or does that cat look a little boxy?

PARTY SHIRT

Repurpose an old t-shirt into a stylish new outfit for Fluffy. T-shirt sleeves are often the perfect size for little kitty bodies—just cut slits for legs, then customize with ribbon, lace, and bows.

Bold colors look great on dark-haired cats.

Materials

- T-shirt with elastic cuffed sleeves

- Ribbon

- Rickrack

- Lace

- Needle and thread

Instructions

1. Cut a sleeve off of the t-shirt.

2. Cut two slits for the cat's legs. The measurements noted in the diagram below should work for most cats, but you may need to adjust the positioning to fit your cat.

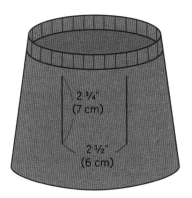

2 ¾"
(7 cm)

2 ½"
(6 cm)

3. Sew the lace around the bottom edge and the rickrack around the top edge. Use the ribbon to tie a bow, then sew to the top of the t-shirt.

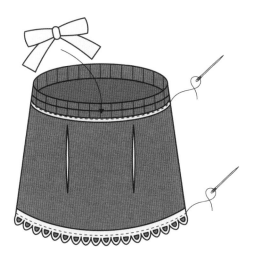

I'm ready to hit the town!

UPCYCLED T-SHIRT

Cut a tube of fabric out of an old thermal t-shirt to create a cute cat costume. Embellish with ribbon and lace to transform your old t-shirt into an extra special outfit for your feline friend.

Materials

- Thermal t-shirt
- Ribbon
- Needle and thread

Does this shirt make me look fat?

Instructions

1. Cut a 6 ½" x 12" (16.5 x 30.5 cm) tube from the two layers of the t-shirt. Fold the top half inside the tube.

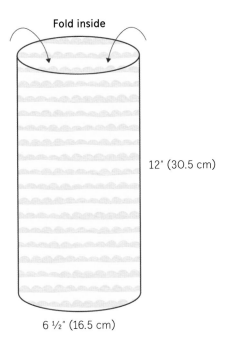

Fold inside

12" (30.5 cm)

6 ½" (16.5 cm)

2. Sew the two layers together around the bottom of the tube.

3. Cut two slits for the cat's legs. The measurements noted in the diagram below should work for most cats, but you may need to adjust the positioning to fit your cat.

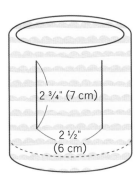

2 ¾" (7 cm)

2 ½" (6 cm)

4. Sew ribbon around the top edge. If desired, use the ribbon to tie bows, then sew them to the top of the t-shirt.

SANTA HAT

Handcraft your cat's very own bright red Santa hat for a cute holiday portrait. This hat is super easy to stitch up—don't forget to top it off with a fuzzy white pompom.

Materials

- Red felt

- White faux shearling fabric

- One 1 ¼" (3 cm) white pompom

- Flat rubber band

Instructions

1. Use the template on page 97 to cut the hat out of red felt. Fold the felt in half and sew together along the straight edge. Trim the tip of the hat just above the seam, being careful not to cut through the stitches.

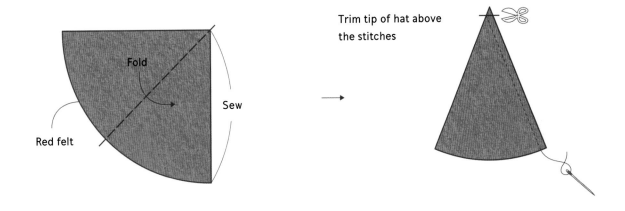

Trim tip of hat above the stitches

Fold

Sew

Red felt

2. Turn the hat right side out. Sew the pompom to the tip of the hat. Sew a strip of faux shearling fabric around the bottom of the hat.

3. Cut a 9 ¾" (25 cm) long piece of rubber band. Sew the ends of the rubber band to the inside of the hat.

RUDOLPH HAT

This reindeer hat is sure to get your cat in the holiday spirit. With just two simple seams, this adorable topper requires very little sewing. Glue felt cutouts to the hat for ears, antlers, eyes, and the quintessential red nose.

Materials

- Brown, orange, red, white, and black felt
- Needle and thread
- Glue

Instructions

1. Use the template on page 95 to cut two head pieces out of brown felt. Sew the two pieces together along the top and bottom.

2. Turn right side out. Use the template on page 95 to cut two ears out of brown felt. Sew the ears to the head following the placement noted on the template.

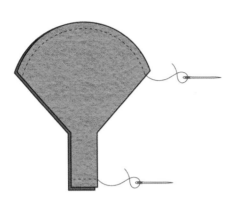

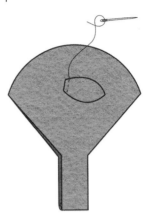

3. Use the templates on page 95 to cut the antlers, nose, and eyes out of felt. Glue the pieces of felt to the head.

Tip: You can also cut slits for your cat's ears (refer to the template on page 95 for placement). If cutting slits, there's no need to adhere the felt reindeer ears.

GHOST HAT

"Trick or treat! Or maybe just treats, please!"
This ghost-themed hat is perfect for Halloween.

Materials

- White, pink, and purple felt

- Two 6" (15 cm) long pieces of white rickrack

- Needle and thread

- Glue

Instructions

1. Use the templates on page 96 to cut the hands and body out of white felt. Sandwich the hands between the two body pieces and sew around the curved edge.

2. Cut two slits for the ears following the placement indicated on the template. These measurements should work for most cats, but you may need to adjust the positioning to fit your cat.

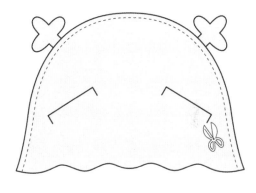

3. Use the templates on page 96 to cut the eyes out of purple felt and the mouth out of pink felt. Glue the felt pieces to the face.

4. Sew the rickrack to the inside of the hat.

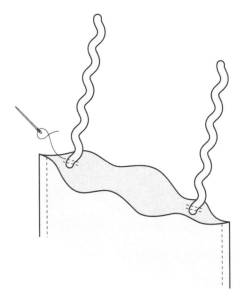

EMPRESS & EMPEROR CROWNS

Does your cat act like royalty? These adorable crowns are perfect for regal cats. Just don't tell them that they are made from toilet paper rolls!

These hats were designed for traditional Japanese holidays, but they work great year-round!

CHILDREN'S DAY FISH HAT

Revered for their determination and strength, fish are a beloved symbol of Children's Day in Japan. Celebrate Children's Day, or your cat's love for fish, with this whimsical hat made from a fluffy striped sock, some felt, and googly eyes.

DUMPLING CAP

This adorable cap was inspired by *mochi*, or rice cakes which are eaten during New Year's celebrations in Japan. Made from a fluffy sock, this little hat will look cute on your cat any day of the year.

Materials for the Empress Crown

- Gold origami paper
- Flower-shaped sequins
- Toilet paper tube
- 8"–10" (20–25 cm) long flat rubber band
- Small beads
- Glue
- Awl

Instructions

1. Cut a 2" (5 cm) long piece of toilet paper tube. Glue the origami paper to the tube. Once the glue is dry, cut the top into a zigzag shape using the template on page 95.

2. Use an awl to punch two holes into the toilet paper tube near the bottom.

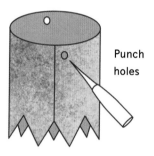

Punch holes

3. Glue the sequins and the beads to the crown.

4. Thread the rubber band through the holes and tie the ends together to create a strap.

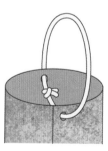

Materials for the Emperor Crown

- Toilet paper tube
- 8"–10" (20-25 cm) long flat rubber band
- Black origami paper
- Sequins
- Small beads
- Glue
- Awl

Instructions

1. Cut a 2" (5 cm) long piece of toilet paper tube. Glue the origami paper to the tube.

Toilet paper tube

Origami paper

2. Use an awl to punch two holes into the toilet paper tube near the bottom.

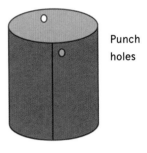

Punch holes

3. Glue the sequins and the beads to the hat. Use the template on page 95 to cut the flap out of black origami paper. Glue the flap to the inside of the tube.

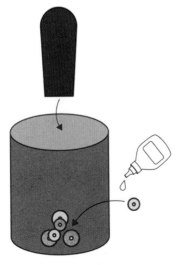

4. Thread the rubber band through the holes and tie the ends together to create a strap.

Materials for the Children's Day Fish Hat

- One marshmallow texture striped sock
- Needle and thread
- Two 1 ¼" (3 cm) googly eyes
- Glue
- Red felt

Instructions

1. Cut an 8" (20 cm) long section of the sock. Cut a 2" (5 cm) tall triangle from the foot end of the sock to create the fins. Turn the sock inside out and sew the sock closed along triangular portion.

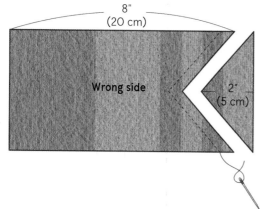

2. Turn right side out. Cut two 1 ½" (4 cm) long slits for your cat's ears and one 2 ¾" (7 cm) long slit for your cat's neck. These measurements should work for most cats, but you may need to adjust the positioning to fit your cat.

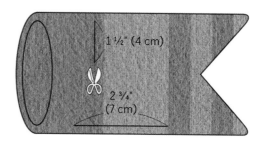

3. Use the templates on page 94 to cut the fins out of red felt. Sew the two dorsal fins together using blanket stitch, then sew to the sock. Sew a pectoral fin to each side of the sock.

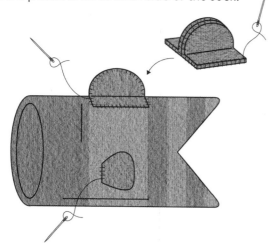

4. Glue the googly eyes to the sock.

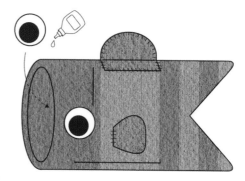

Materials for the Dumpling Cap

- One marshmallow texture white sock
- One ¾" (2 cm) pompom
- Light green felt
- 6"-8" (15-20 cm) long flat rubber band
- Cotton stuffing
- Needle and thread
- Glue

Instructions

1. Cut the foot off of the sock.

2. Fill the foot of the sock with stuffing. Sew around the opening, then pull the thread taut to squeeze the sock closed. Tie a knot and trim the thread ends. Sew around the middle of the stuffed sock, then squeeze into a whipped cream shape. Tie a knot and trim the thread ends.

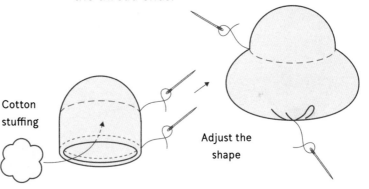

Cotton stuffing

Adjust the shape

3. Cut a small leaf out of green felt. Glue the leaf to the pompom, then glue the pompom to the top of the stuffed sock.

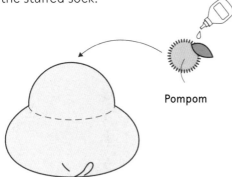

Pompom

4. Sew the ends of the rubber band to the sides of the stuffed sock.

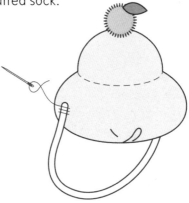

KITTY KERCHIEF

This stylish bandana was designed for cats who love to accessorize! It even features a special spot for a name tag in case your cat ever goes missing.

Pastel colors look great on light-haired cats.

Materials

- ⅓ yard (0.3 m) of polka dot fabric

- 10" (26 cm) of white lace

- One ⅝" x 1" (1.5 x 2.5 cm) piece of hook and loop tape

- Clear vinyl

- White card stock

Instructions

1. Cut A and B from the polka dot fabric. Cut the clear vinyl to 1 ¼" x 1 ½" (3 x 4 cm).

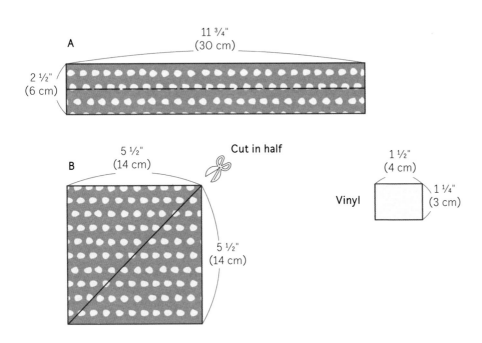

A

11 ¾"
(30 cm)

2 ½"
(6 cm)

B

5 ½"
(14 cm)

Cut in half

5 ½"
(14 cm)

Vinyl

1 ½"
(4 cm)

1 ¼"
(3 cm)

2. Sew around three sides to attach the clear vinyl to one of the B pieces. Write your cat's name and your contact info on the card stock. Trim the card stock and insert into the vinyl pocket.

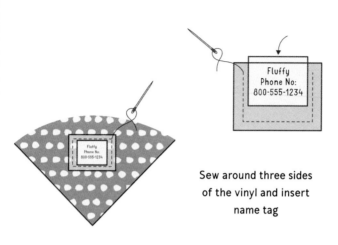

Sew around three sides
of the vinyl and insert
name tag

3. Align the two B pieces with right sides together. Sew along the two equal edges of the triangle, then turn right side out.

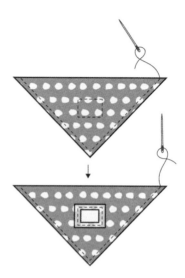

4. Fold the two long edges of A over ¼" (5 mm). Fold the two short edges over ¾" (2 cm). Align the straight edge of B along the center of A, then fold A in half along the center. Sew around all four sides of A.

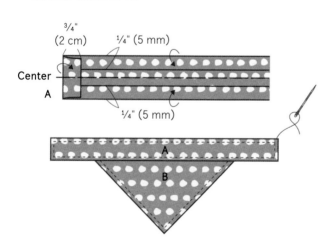

5. Sew the hook and loop tape to A. Make sure to sew one piece to the wrong side and one piece to the right side. Sew the lace to A.

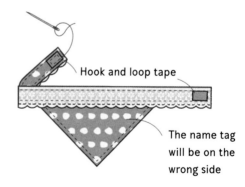

Hook and loop tape

The name tag will be on the wrong side

KITTY KIRIGAMI

The elegant cat silhouette makes an excellent design for *kirigami*, which is the art of papercutting. Use these motifs for greeting cards, scrapbooks, or window decorations.

In my opinion, you can never have too much cat décor!

Materials

For A

- Orange scrapbook paper
- Gray felt
- White rickrack
- Glue
- Markers

For B

- Teal scrapbook paper
- 4 ½" (11.8 cm) square of light green origami paper
- White lace
- Glue
- Craft knife

For C & D

- 6" (15 cm) square of red or light blue origami paper
- Craft knife

Instructions for A

1. Fold the felt in half. Use the template on page 99 to cut the cat out of felt, positioning the template on the fold.

2. Fold the scrapbook paper in half to form into a card. Glue the felt cat to the card. Glue the rickrack to the felt cat to create a collar. Use the markers to add text and illustrations.

Felt

Instructions for B

1. Fold the origami paper in half, then fold into eighths. Use the template on page 99 to cut the cat out of origami paper, positioning the template on the folds.

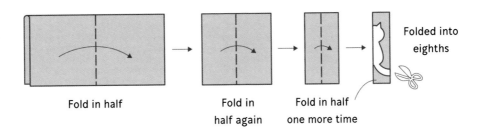

Fold in half   Fold in half again   Fold in half one more time   Folded into eighths

2. Glue the cats and the lace to the scrapbook paper. Fold in half to form into a card.

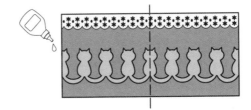

Instructions for C & D

1. Fold the origami paper into twelfths. Use the templates on page 100 to cut the designs out of the paper.

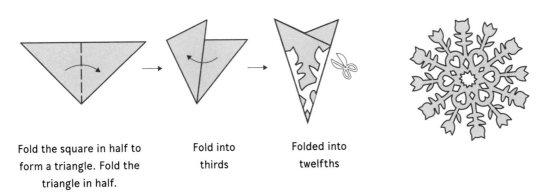

Fold the square in half to form a triangle. Fold the triangle in half.   Fold into thirds   Folded into twelfths

CAT SCRAPBOOKS

Commemorate your favorite moments with your cat using these special cat scrapbooks. Decorate the cover of a store bought notebook or photo album with lace, fabric, and decorative paper, then insert your favorite photos.

Materials

- Notebook or photo album
- Cat photos
- Scrapbook paper
- Fabric
- Felt
- Ribbon
- Lace
- Buttons
- Glue

Instructions

1. Glue the scrapbook paper, fabric, ribbon, and lace to the notebook or photo album cover to create a background.

2. Cut the templates on page 97 out of felt and glue to the background. Glue cat photos, buttons, ribbon, and any other desired decorations to the background.

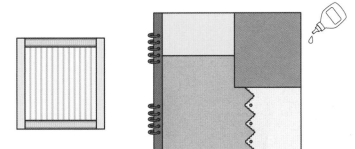

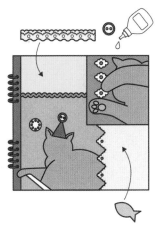

Tip: To take cat photos with a sense of movement, I recommend shooting several photos continuously. This will allow you to capture your cat in action!

CAT STATIONERY

Elevate your personal correspondence with cat-themed stationery.
Glue cat photos to colorfully printed scrapbook paper to create your
own postcards and notecards.

Materials

- Cat photos

- Scrapbook paper

- Glue

- Colored pens

Instructions

1. Glue cat photos to the scrapbook paper.

2. Use the templates on page 98 to cut speech bubbles out of scrapbook paper. Use the colored pens to write funny captions.

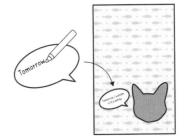

Tip: When you take a great cat photo, I recommend making several copies. This will allow you to play around with the layout and sizing for different designs.

CAT CAMEO FRAMES

Keep your cat close to your heart wherever you go with these fun felt photo frames. Attach a ribbon to wear the photo as a necklace or use it as bookmark.

I'm just so photogenic!

Materials

- Cat photo
- Felt
- Ribbon
- Glue
- Tape
- Needle and thread

Color Combination Chart

	A	B	C
Felt	Light pink Dark pink	Cream Tan	Light blue Blue Purple
Ribbon	Red	Yellow	Light blue

Instructions

1. Use the template on page 99 to cut two cat heads out of felt. Fold one of the pieces in half and cut out the window.

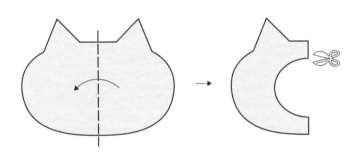

2. Use the templates on page 99 to cut out the remaining felt pieces for your desired design. Glue the felt pieces to the cat head with the window.

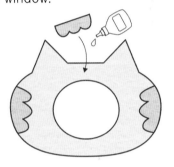

3. Cut out your cat photo. Tape the ribbon to the back of the photo.

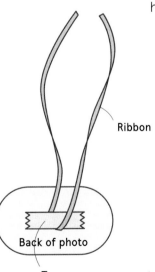

1 ½"
(3.5 cm)

1 ½"
(4 cm)

Back of photo

Tape

Ribbon

4. Sandwich the photo in between the two felt cat heads. Sew the two pieces of felt together.

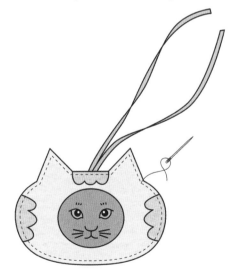

CATTITUDE T-SHIRTS

Create custom graphic tees using iron-on transfer paper and images of your cat. For a bold look, take close-up photos of your cat in action.

Materials

- T-shirt
- White paper
- Iron-on transfer paper
- Cat photos
- Iron
- Glue

Instructions

1. Glue your cat photos to a sheet of white paper. Copy this sheet onto a piece of iron-on transfer paper. Mounting the photos on white paper first will prevent you from wasting iron-on transfer paper.

2. Cut the photos out of the iron-on transfer paper. Position the photos on the shirt.

3. Follow the manufacturer's instructions to transfer the photos to the shirt.

Where's mine?

MODCAT PLACEMAT SET

Inspired by cat silhouettes, this mod placemat and coaster set
is perfect for entertaining. Have fun mixing different fabrics to
create a one-of-a-kind table setting.

Materials for Placemat

- ¼ yard (0.25 m) of brown polka dot fabric

- 14" x 18" (35 x 45 cm) of beige fabric

- Sewing machine

Instructions

1. Use the templates on page 101 to cut the ear and tail pieces out of brown polka dot fabric. For each ear and the tail, align the pieces with right sides together and sew, leaving the straight edge open.

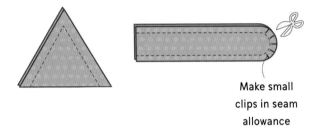

Make small clips in seam allowance

2. Turn right side out. Fold the fabric in ⅜" (1 cm) along the open edge, then sew closed.

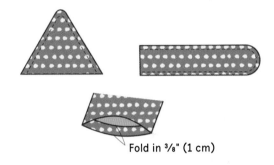

Fold in ⅜" (1 cm)

3. Fold each edge of the beige fabric over ¼" (5 mm) twice. Sew around all four edges.

4. Align the ears and tail underneath the beige fabric and sew in place.

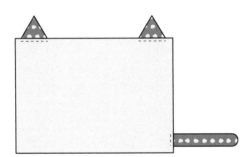

Materials for Coasters

- Two 4" x 4" (10 x 10 cm) pieces each of brown and pink polka dot fabrics

- Brown felt

- Sewing machine or needle and thread

Instructions

1. Use the templates on page 101 to cut the ears and tail out of felt. Align the two pieces of polka dot fabric with right sides together with the ears and tail sandwiched in between. Sew around all four sides, leaving an opening.

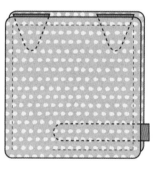

2. Turn right side out. Fold the fabric in ⅜" (1 cm) along the open edge, then sew closed.

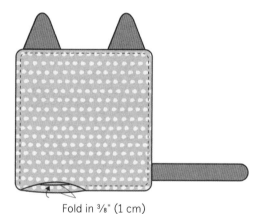

Fold in ⅜" (1 cm)

This tableware is great for entertaining!

PAWPRINT PILLOWS

Incorporate your love of cats into your home décor with these pawprint pillows. Made with a combination of felt and fleece, these pillows are so cozy that you may catch your cat snuggling up to them during naptime.

Use fleece to make this pillow extra cozy!

Materials

- ¾ yard (0.7 m) of pink or light green fleece

- Brown or pink felt

- Cotton stuffing

- Sewing machine

- Needle and thread

Instructions

1. Use the templates on pages 102–103 to cut the pillow pieces out of fleece and the pawprint pieces out of felt. Align the pawprint pieces on top of one of the pillow pieces. Zigzag stitch the pawprint to the pillow.

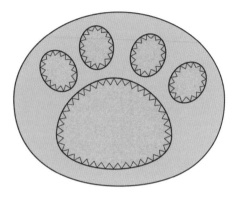

2. Align the two pillow pieces with right sides together. Sew around the pillow, leaving a 2" (5 cm) opening.

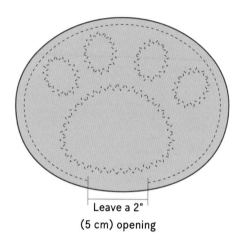

Leave a 2" (5 cm) opening

3. Turn the pillow right side out. Fill with stuffing.

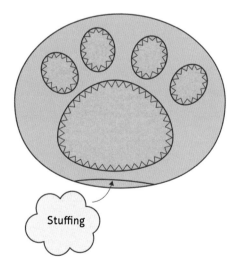

Stuffing

4. Hand sew the opening closed.

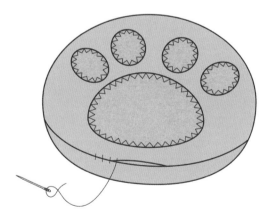

SNUGGLE CAT

Every cat needs a friend to cuddle with during naptime! This stuffed toy is simple to make since it uses store-bought gloves instead of small pieces of fabric, which can be difficult to sew.

Meet my snuggle buddy...his name is Mittens!

Materials

- One pair of red knit gloves

- 16" (40 cm) of ribbon

- Two ⅜" x ½" (9 x 12 mm) eye buttons

- One ¼" (7 mm) nose

- Cotton stuffing

- Needle and thread

Instructions

1. On one of the gloves, fold the three middle fingers into the hand. Fold half of the pinkie finger and half of the thumb in to create triangular ears. Sew the two layers of the glove together to secure this shape in place.

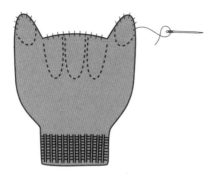

2. Fold the wrist into the hand. Fill the glove with stuffing.

3. Cut the thumb off of the other glove. Insert stuffing into the four fingers and the portion of the hand beneath the dotted line.

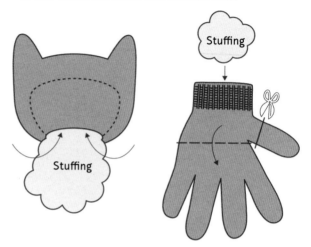

Stuffing

Stuffing

4. Pinch the pinkie and index fingers to create arms and sew in place. Fold the fabric in ⅜" (1 cm) along the open edge of the thumb. Sew it to the back of the glove to create a tail.

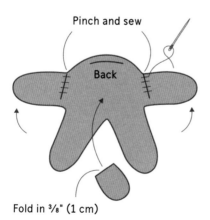

Pinch and sew

Back

Fold in ⅜" (1 cm)

5. Sew the head to the body. Tie the ribbon into a bow and sew to the neck. Glue the eyes and nose to the face.

CAT WRAP POUCHES

Make a few basic origami folds to transform boring old bandanas and handkerchiefs into feline-themed fabric pouches. Personalize your pouch with a friendly face by gluing on some felt cutouts and embroidering cute little whiskers. These Japanese *furoshiki*-inspired pouches make excellent lunch bags or gift bags for delivering homemade baked goods.

Materials

For A

- One 19 ¾" x 19 ¾" (50 x 50 cm) navy handkerchief

- White felt

- White embroidery floss

- Glue

- Needle and thread

For B

- One 14 ¼" x 14 ¼" (36 x 36 cm) white handkerchief

- Pink felt

- Red embroidery floss

- Glue

- Needle and thread

Instructions

1. Fold the handkerchief in half to form a rectangle. Fold along the dashed line to create a 90° angle as shown. Rotate the fabric so the folded edge is straight.

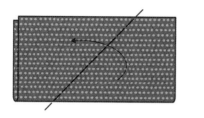

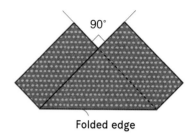

90°

Folded edge

2. Fold each pointed section to create the ears.

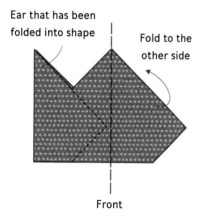

Ear that has been folded into shape

Fold to the other side

Front

3. Sew the fabric together on the back and bottom.

Back

4. Pinch each corner to form a triangle. Fold the triangles and sew to the bottom.

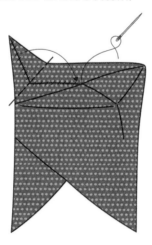

5. Sew the fabric together on the front. Use the templates on page 101 to cut the nose and eyes out of felt. Glue the felt pieces to the face. Embroider the whiskers.

TISSUE BOX COZY

Celebrate your inner cat lady with this tissue box cover made from a washcloth. Use felt cutouts to create a feline face and tail, then embellish with decorative ribbon. Both functional and adorable, this sweet little project will bring cheer to any room.

Materials

- One light green washcloth (the one used here measured 13" [33 cm] square)

- 16" (40 cm) of ribbon (for hanging)

- 14" (36 cm) each of gingham ribbon and black rickrack

- Blue and green felt

- One ⅝" x 1" (1.5 x 2.5 cm) piece of hook and loop tape

- Glue

- Needle and thread

Instructions

1. Fold the washcloth into three sections (the middle section should be twice as large as the outside sections).

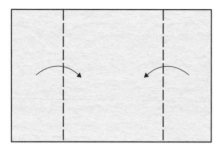

2. Sew the washcloth together along the back, leaving a gap in the middle. Sew the washcloth closed along the top. Next, sew the two layers together in a curved shape, slightly below the top. Pull taut to create the pointed ears.

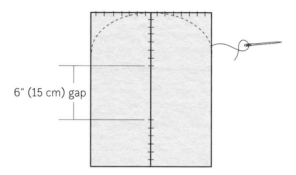

6" (15 cm) gap

3. Sew one half of the hook and loop tape to the outside bottom and the other half to the inside bottom. Fold the bottom into shape (just like you would when wrapping a gift box) and insert the tissue box.

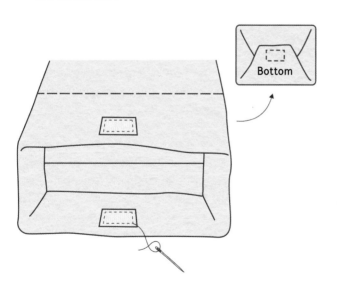

Bottom

4. Use the templates on page 100 to cut the eyes, nose, whiskers, and tail out of felt. Glue the felt pieces to the cat. Sew the rickrack and ribbon to the washcloth. Fold the 16" (40 cm) long ribbon in half and sew to the top.

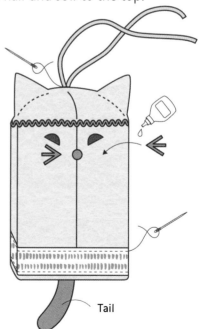

Tail

FULL-SIZE TEMPLATES

Catnip Mouse

Shown on page 6

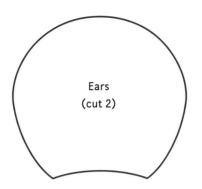

Ears
(cut 2)

Eyes
(cut 2)

Nose
(cut 1)

Fan-tastic Teaser

Shown on page 10

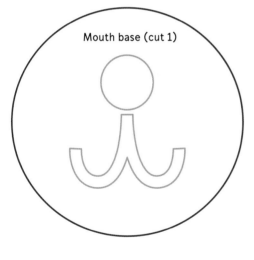

Mouth base (cut 1)

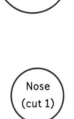

Eyes
(cut 2)

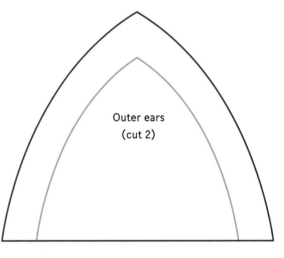

Outer ears
(cut 2)

Nose
(cut 1)

Mouth (cut 1)

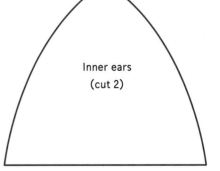

Inner ears
(cut 2)

Crinkle Critters

Shown on page 12

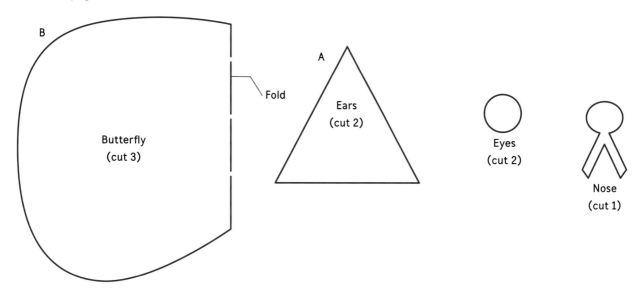

B

Butterfly
(cut 3)

Fold

A

Ears
(cut 2)

Eyes
(cut 2)

Nose
(cut 1)

Go Fish Teaser

Shown on page 16

Eyes
(cut 2)

Dorsal fin
(cut 1)

Pectoral fins
(cut 2)

Stomach fins
(cut 2)

Convertible Cat Bed

Shown on page 34

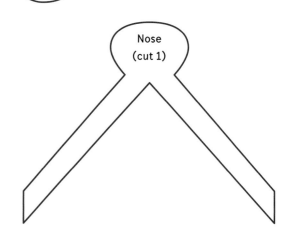

Eyes
(cut 2)

Nose
(cut 1)

The Cat Chateau

Shown on page 22

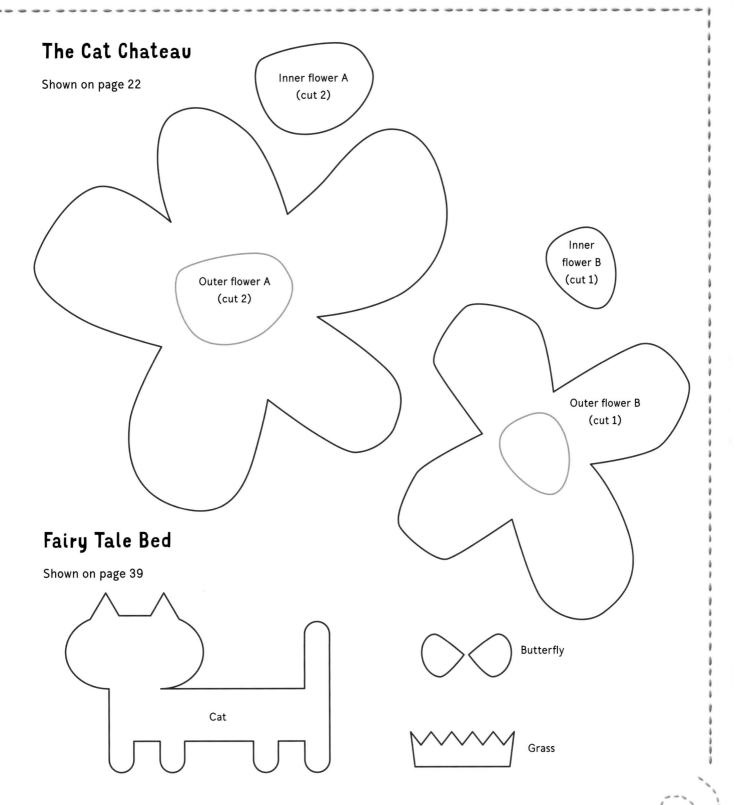

Inner flower A
(cut 2)

Outer flower A
(cut 2)

Inner flower B
(cut 1)

Outer flower B
(cut 1)

Fairy Tale Bed

Shown on page 39

Cat

Butterfly

Grass

Tidy Cat Storage Box

Shown on page 46

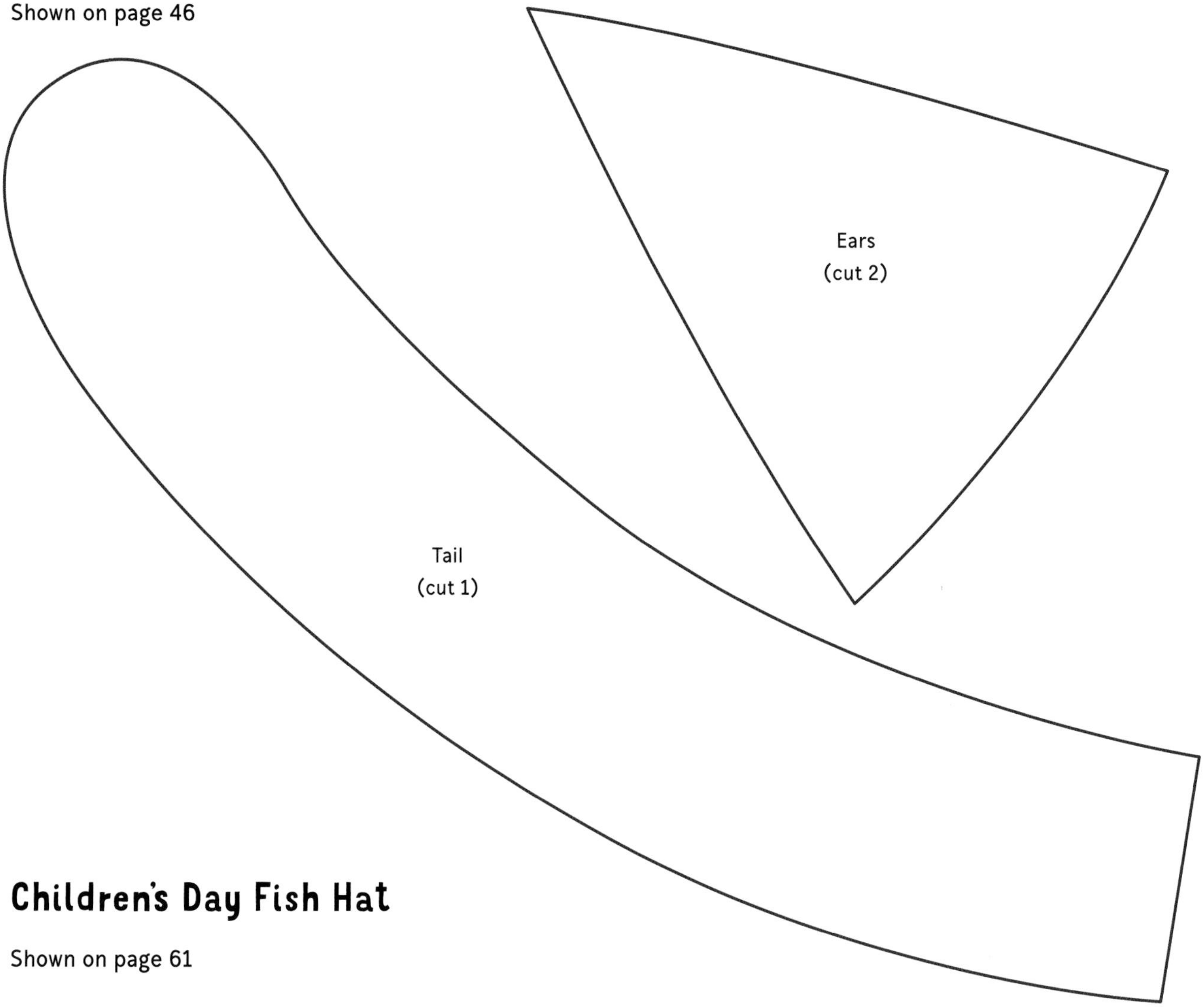

Ears
(cut 2)

Tail
(cut 1)

Children's Day Fish Hat

Shown on page 61

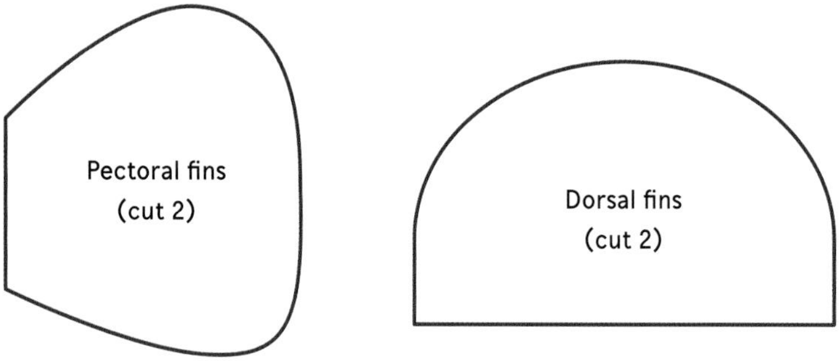

Pectoral fins
(cut 2)

Dorsal fins
(cut 2)

Rudolph Hat

Shown on page 56

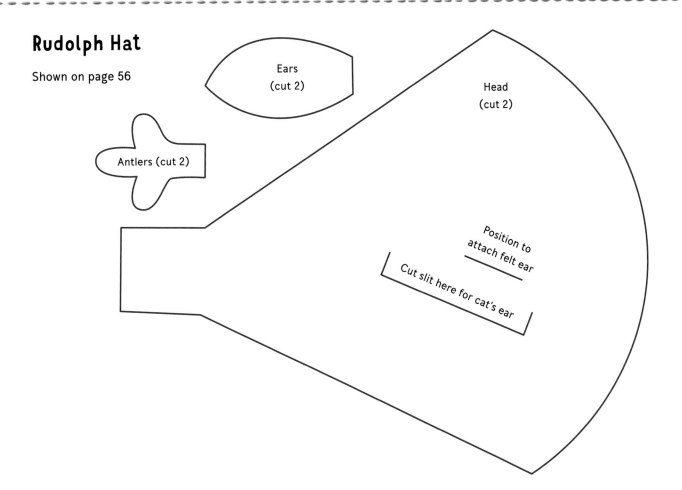

Ears
(cut 2)

Head
(cut 2)

Antlers (cut 2)

Position to
attach felt ear

Cut slit here for cat's ear

Empress & Emperor Crowns

Shown on page 60

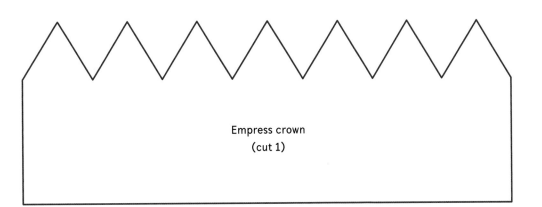

Empress crown
(cut 1)

Emperor
crown flap
(cut 1)

Ghost Hat

Shown on page 58

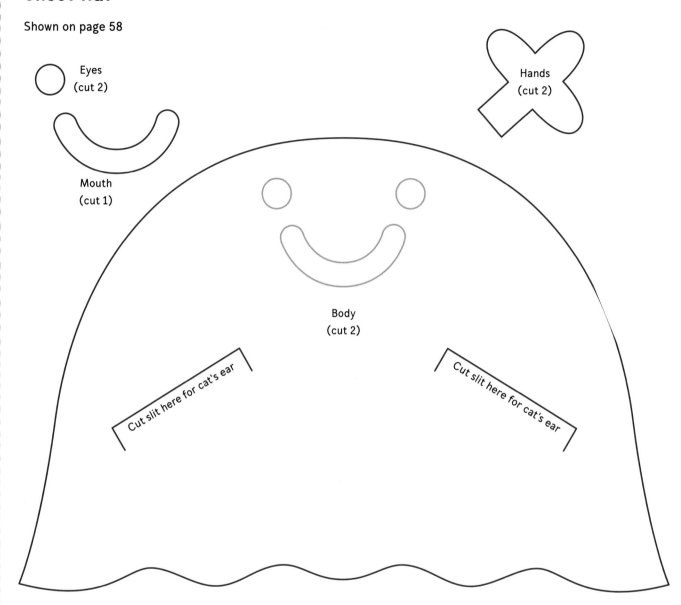

Eyes
(cut 2)

Hands
(cut 2)

Mouth
(cut 1)

Body
(cut 2)

Cut slit here for cat's ear

Cut slit here for cat's ear

Cat Scrapbooks

Shown on page 72

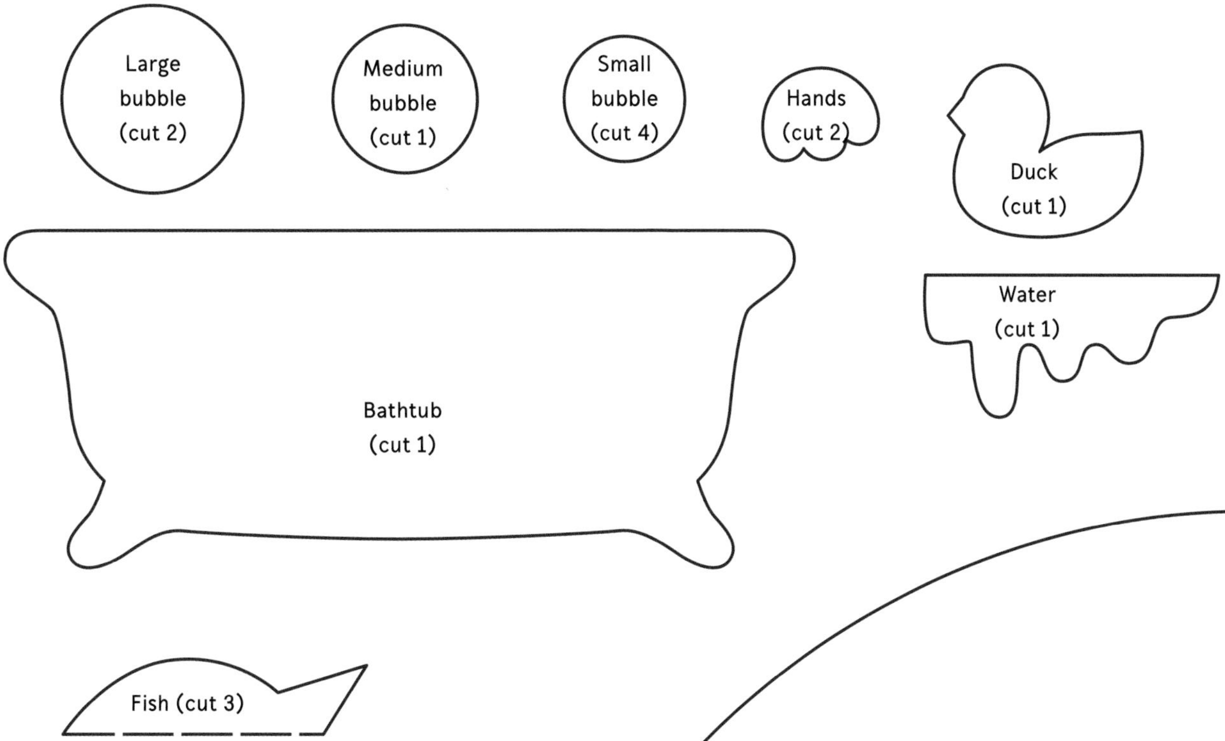

Large bubble (cut 2)

Medium bubble (cut 1)

Small bubble (cut 4)

Hands (cut 2)

Duck (cut 1)

Water (cut 1)

Bathtub (cut 1)

Fish (cut 3)

Santa Hat

Shown on page 54

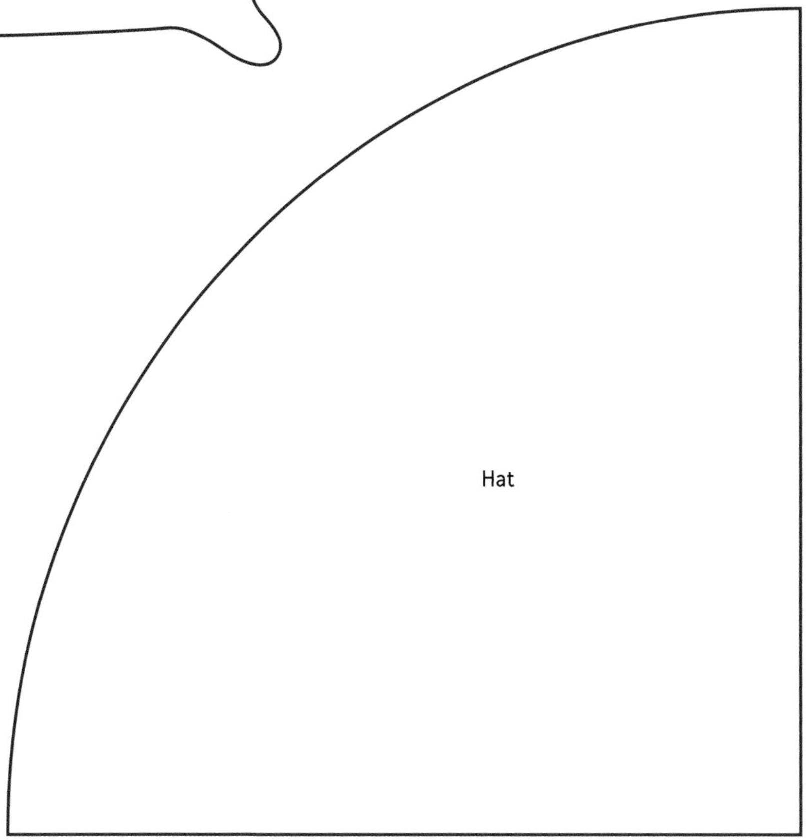

Hat

Cat Stationery

Shown on page 74

Cat Cameo Frames

Shown on page 76

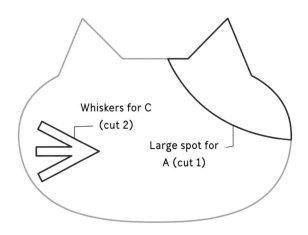

Whiskers for C
(cut 2)

Large spot for
A (cut 1)

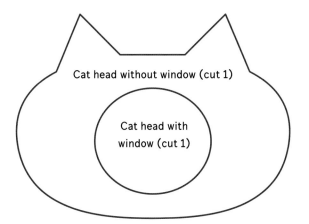

Cat head without window (cut 1)

Cat head with
window (cut 1)

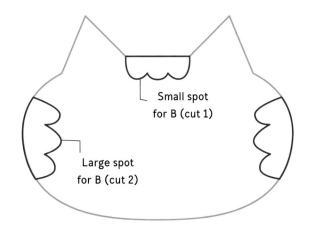

Small spot
for B (cut 1)

Large spot
for B (cut 2)

Kitty Kirigami

Shown on page 69

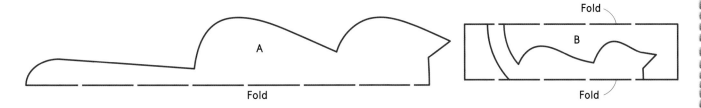

A

Fold

Fold

B

Fold

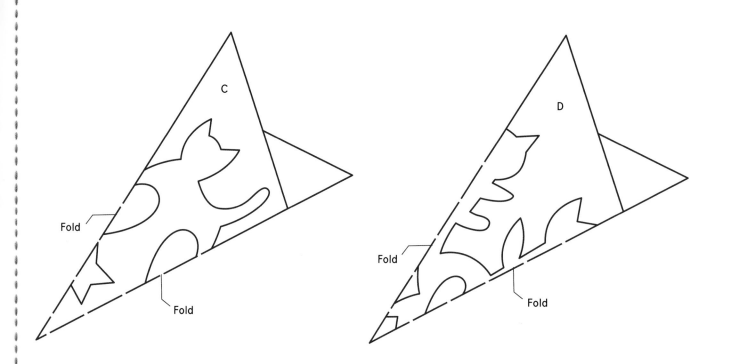

C

D

Fold

Fold

Fold

Fold

Tissue Box Cozy

Shown on page 89

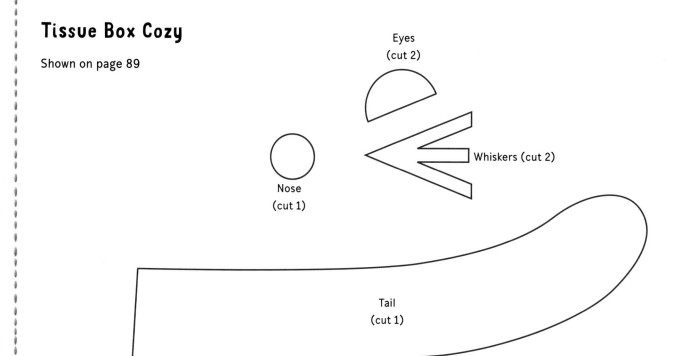

Eyes
(cut 2)

Whiskers (cut 2)

Nose
(cut 1)

Tail
(cut 1)

Modcat Placemat Set

Shown on page 80

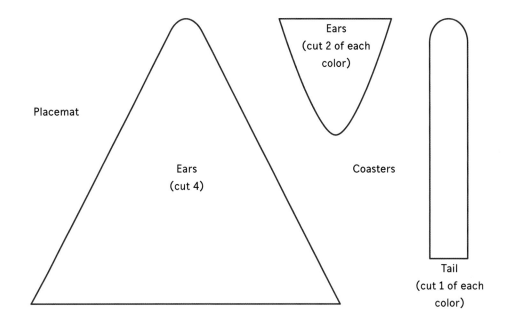

Tail
(cut 2)

Placemat

Ears
(cut 4)

Ears
(cut 2 of each
color)

Coasters

Tail
(cut 1 of each
color)

Cat Wrap Pouches

Shown on page 87

A

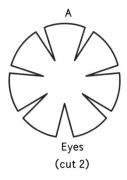

Eyes
(cut 2)

Nose
(cut 1)

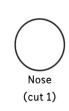

B

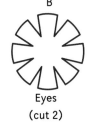

Eyes
(cut 2)

Nose
(cut 1)

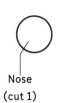

Pawprint Pillows

Shown on page 83

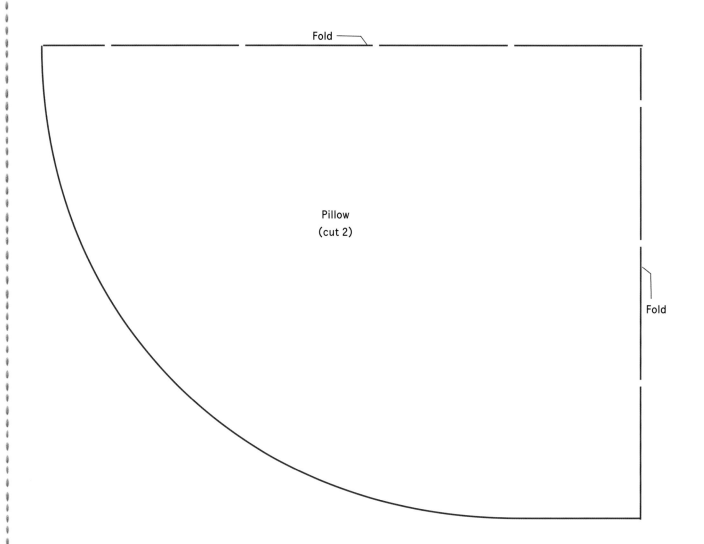

Fold

Pillow
(cut 2)

Fold

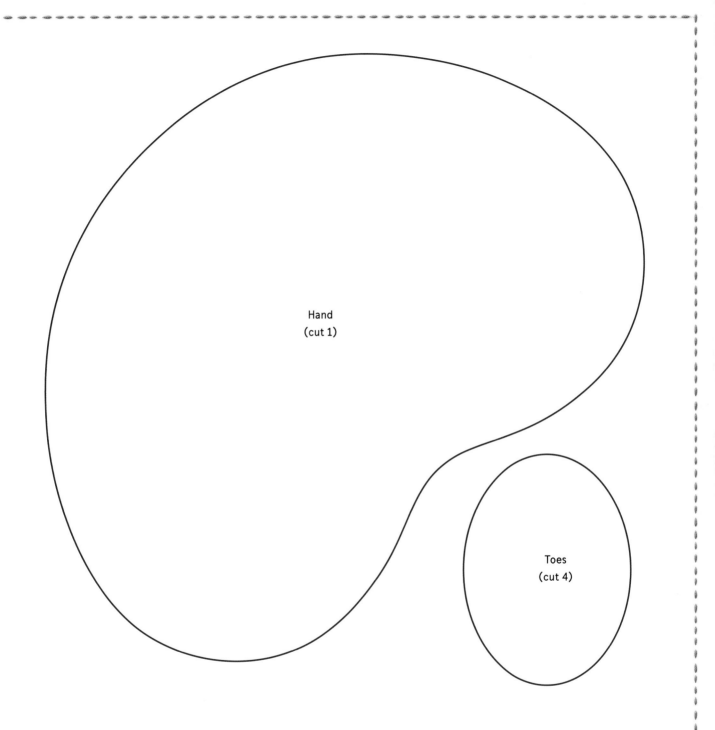

Hand
(cut 1)

Toes
(cut 4)

ABOUT THE AUTHOR

Mariko Ishikawa previously worked as a designer for a toy company, as well as for a production company specializing in children's videos. She now works as a freelance handicraft artist and has published multiple books in Japan. She is a cat lover who shares her home with seven cats.

The Ishikawa Family

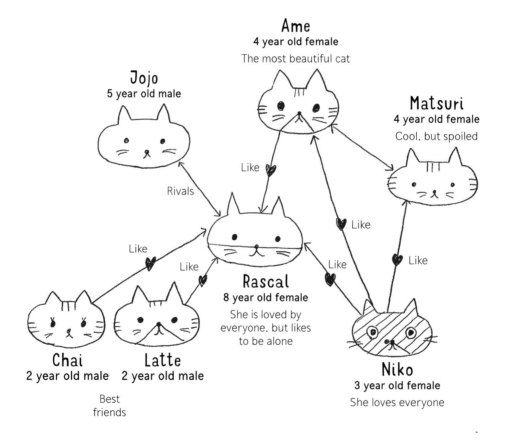

Ame
4 year old female
The most beautiful cat

Jojo
5 year old male

Matsuri
4 year old female
Cool, but spoiled

Like

Rivals

Like

Like

Like

Like

Like

Like

Like

Rascal
8 year old female
She is loved by everyone, but likes to be alone

Chai
2 year old male

Latte
2 year old male

Best friends

Niko
3 year old female
She loves everyone